MAKING DREAMS COME TRUE

Merry Christmas Pez!
Happy Dreaming for
all the Robbos in
2008!
Love & Laughter

MAKING DREAMS COME TRUE

*Simple visualisations and practical exercises
to help children set and achieve goals.*

FOR PARENTS, TEACHERS AND CHILDREN
AGED ONE TO INFINITY

VICKI BENNETT

Illustrations by Penny Lovelock

Gazebo

*FOR FIVE WONDERFUL WOMEN - MY GIRLS
CASSIE, ELLIE, GALEA, ROSALIND, AND TAMMIE,
THE VERY BEST DREAM MAKERS*

First published in Australia and New Zealand in 1996 by
Hodder Headline Australia Pty Limited

This edition published in Great Britain in 1999 by
Gazebo Publishing, PO Box 1579, Stratford-upon-Avon CV37 8ZL

Copyright © Vicki Bennett, 1996
Illustrations Copyright © Penny Lovelock, 1996
Forms Copyright © Vicki Bennett and David Eccles, 1996-99

This book is copyright. No part may be stored or reproduced by any process without prior written permission from the publisher.

A CIP catalogue record for this book is available from the British Library.

ISBN 0 9535086 0 9

Author photograph courtesy of Martin Johnston, Brisbane News

Printed by Ebenezer Baylis, Worcester

*As a child, I created a safe place to dream as I was going to sleep.
I created a special garden in my imagination
and it has helped me in my life
to solve problems and to feel good about myself.
I shared this place at bedtime with my children,
and it has helped them, and thousands of other children who use it,
to learn and love.*

VICKI BENNETT

Contents

Making Dreams Come True   9

HOW TO MAKE DREAMS COME TRUE
- ★ *Visualisation*
- ★ *Goalsetting*

For Adults   15

FOR PARENTS
- ★ *Using this book*
- ★ *Parents and visualisation*
- ★ *Children and visualisation*

FOR TEACHERS
- ★ *Regular visualisation in the classroom*

All Together Now   25

SUCCESS STORIES
- ★ *Tammie*
- ★ *Cassie*
- ★ *Ben*
- ★ *Sally*

Now It's Your Turn   37

HOW VISUALISATION WORKS
- ★ *People and visualisation*

SECRET GARDEN

WOODLANDS HEALING

THE MAGIC CAVE OF FRIENDS

THE BEACH AND THE HEALING WHITE LIGHT

THE LIBRARY OF LEARNING

FLYING IN THE CLOUDS

THE PINK BUBBLE

Achieving Your Dreams   69

GOALSETTING
- ★ *Kylie's Goals*

HOW TO SET GOALS

THINGS TO REMEMBER WHEN MAKING GOALS
- ★ *Sandy's Story*
- ★ *Revising Goals*
- ★ *Bobby's Goals*

YOUR TURN
- ★ *Your Goals*

Your Own Special Place for Dreams   93

KEEP ON DREAMING

Making Dreams Come True

It's never too late to have a happy childhood.
TOM ROBBINS

How to Make Dreams Come True

This is a book for children and grown-ups to share. Through creative visualisation and goalsetting you can make your dreams, and assist in making your children's dreams, come true.

Visualisation is an effective tool for children and adults alike. Children use their imagination for creative learning and play, but often adults don't understand children's imaginary friends, or their intricate and complicated games. This is because adults have forgotten, because they have grown up. Reach for the child within to keep visualisation alive in your imagination; it is a valuable tool that can be used throughout your life, as children, as teenagers, and as adults.

Adults can learn an enormous amount from children because children's imaginations are so vivid and alive. Children are positive by nature and don't think of reasons why they can't do things, or why things can't be changed - they just go ahead.

In a child's imagination, there are no limitations or boundaries.

Visualisation

Visualisation is creating vivid picture stories in your imagination of what you desire to happen in the future and thinking about it regularly. It is a dream that you activate in your mind while you're still awake.

Choose a time when you can allow your imagination to reign uninterrupted - before going to bed is an ideal time. Begin setting the scene by choosing a place where you feel comfortable - an imaginary place in your mind, perhaps a garden or wood. The selection of the right place is important because you deserve the best and you will be picturing the fine details of your place before beginning to imagine the action or the feeling you want to achieve.

Visualisation is a valuable process because it creates a wonderfully unlimited place in your imagination for both children and adults to retreat to when solving problems. Creating and visiting it is a calming tool where you can let go of fears. It provides a safe place for you to visit when you need comfort. It creates an opportunity to let go of the past and move into the future, and is a place where you can be non-judgemental, forgiving and tolerant. It is a place of active imagination as well as a haven.

It is a place that can also be used in the turbulent and challenging adolescent years, as visualisation draws from inside a person's imagination without the need of anything artificial, outside that person, to solve problems or allay fears.

It also stimulates creativity. Through visualisation, you can access your creative mind and find many solutions for day-to-day problems.

Goalsetting

Goalsetting is the second part of making dreams come true. It is the key to successful visualisation. Setting your goals realistically before beginning the creative visualisation process actually helps you choose the actions you need to perform to make your dreams become reality.

Goalsetting offers a perfect balance between the imagination and action, or the dream and the practical result. It gives you a framework to allow your imagination to run free. Your creativity is activated through the visualisation exercises, and your more active analytical nature is activated by the goalsetting exercises.

When you have become comfortable with the visualisation process, your imagination will have ignited your dreams.

You then begin to structure them more through the goalsetting process, described in the section "Achieving Your Dreams" on page 69. As you set your goals, you write them down and draw a picture of the desired result. You decide what actions to take to achieve your dream and set a date when you hope that your dream will have come true.

The action of planning and writing your goals, as much as the imagination, contributes to the achievement of that dream.

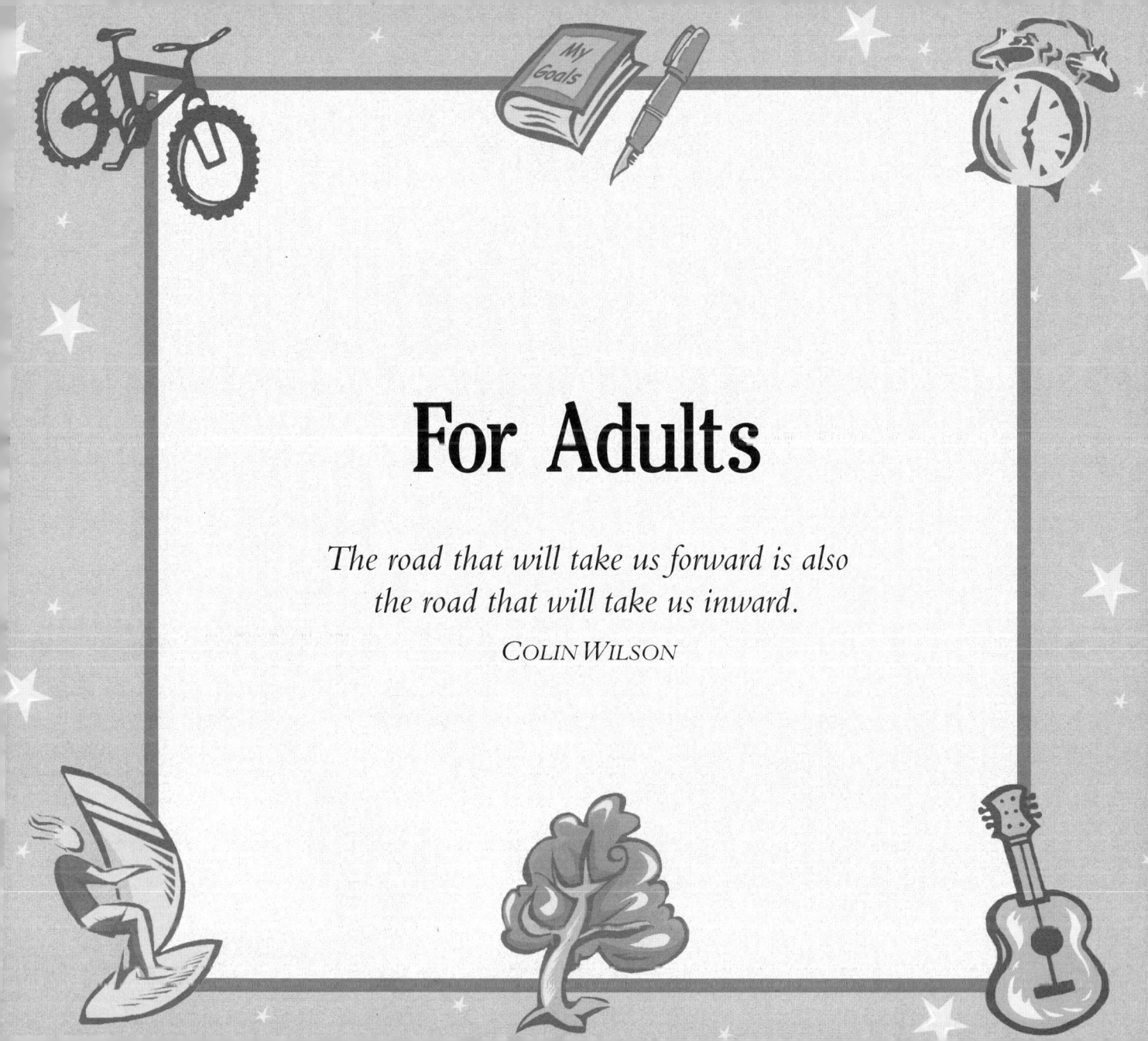

For Adults

The road that will take us forward is also the road that will take us inward.

COLIN WILSON

For Parents

Children who use visualisation regularly tend to be healthy, with a keen concentration, and the ability to take responsibility for their actions. They become very creative.

Sometimes children need a quiet place of their own where nothing goes wrong. They can use their imagination to find this special place. They may imagine a garden, a beach, a cave, a river bank, a wood, or another "make believe" place that could be special for them.

Visualisation creates a wonderful environment for both adults and children to grow and to learn. By teaching children to imagine a positive place to solve problems, you will help to put their young minds to rest. If used at bedtime, children will go on to peaceful sleep after a visualisation exercise.

Some children will already know about using their imagination by visualising. Visualisation is dreaming with your eyes closed, while you are awake. It is seeing a mental picture of what it is you want to happen.

If your imagination is constantly reminded of your wish or desire, the dream eventually becomes real and you achieve your goal. That's why the

"Achieving Your Dreams" section on goalsetting (page 70) is an important part of creating the future, as it allows children to use both sides of their brain to create the future they desire. The creative side (right brain function) is activated through the visualisation exercises, and the action side (left brain function) is activated by the goalsetting exercise.

So when you have shown your child or children the creative process through the visualisation chapters, it is important they commit themselves to their dream by writing down their goals, deciding what they will do to make them come true and when they want them to happen. Once they have written that down, encourage them to draw a picture of their visualised special place, including in that drawing what they wish to achieve (their goal or goals).

Then, when they are ready for sleep (a perfect time to use visualisation as a tool), read aloud the visualisation exercises in this book to your children.

Using this book

This book is divided into sections - the first two sections, "Making Dreams Come True" and "For Adults" are directed towards adults. The next part of the book can be shared by adults and children, or some children may read it for themselves.

In the section "All Together Now", there are diagrams and illustrations of each child's goals. While you may look at them with your child, do not spend time on them until you have read the section on goalsetting called "Achieving Your Dreams".

"Now It's Your Turn" gives you and your child the vehicle to start dreaming by giving practical visualisation exercises to do together or, when the child is ready, on their own.

Parents and visualisation

Parents tell me that after a busy day of work, "going to their garden" with their children relaxes them also and rejuvenates their sometimes flagging spirit, enabling them to spend fresh, quality time with their partners.

One mother told me of how much her husband looked forward to the visualisation exercises with his children every night, and how he became a transformed man, serene and calm after visiting his own "secret cave" with his children at their bedtime.

Children and visualisation

There are several visualisations in this book. Select the ones with your children that suit their needs at the time. Each exercise has a different theme and different focus, for children to learn many things and build their confidence.

When you teach your children to set goals and to see themselves achieving these goals in their imagination, you will share the pleasure of empowering your children with a valuable life skill. You will experience the joy of hearing your child, at bedtime, saying, "Please, take me to my secret place".

For Teachers

Goalsetting and visualisation have many benefits in the classroom. They provide a focus for children to relax and to quieten their minds. They create a non-threatening environment where children and teachers can set joint goals. They provide an additional means to help very active or disruptive children to achieve their potential.

Visualisation exercises are a very successful method for enhancing creativity in children. After a 10 to 15 minute visualisation, a child's concentration is greatly enhanced, making the next period of learning very effective. Visualisation also increases physical and mental well-being in children.

This technique is also transferable to sports, hobbies and relationships. It becomes a self-management technique for children that many will take up and apply for themselves outside of school.

Together, visualisation and goalsetting provide a wonderful vehicle for children to learn to use both functions of their brain, their left brain (analytical/action) and their right (creative/dream). Children might best sit or lie on the floor and close their eyes so that they can access their dream or their goal in comfort and peace.

Try beginning with the "Secret Garden" visualisation on page 40, as it gives children the chance to use their imaginations vividly. This visualisation lasts about 8 to 10 minutes. Read this visualisation slowly, allowing pauses between ideas so children have the chance to build their pictures in their own imagination.

When you ask them to open their eyes, children will begin to use their left brain function. The left brain function creates the goals and the action plan. Follow the plan outlined for goalsetting in "Achieving Your Dreams" on pages 70-72 to help children determine their goals, in their order of importance, and to write them down.

Then the children determine what actions they should take to achieve each of their goals and set a timeframe of when they want to achieve them. Finally, ask the children to draw their goal or dream. When they draw their dream into picture form, they are using both brain functions effectively.

Regular visualisation in the classroom

Then, on a daily basis, maybe after lunch or just before a lesson where you need full concentration, ask the children to lie down and visualise their goals, their dreams.

Doing this on a regular basis has an amazingly positive effect on children. Teachers also benefit by becoming more goal-oriented and focused as well.

Visualisation can also be used to deal positively with exams, assignments, or any other goals or targets. Some visualisation exercises in this book are ideal for particular aspects of school life:

- ★ "The Library of Learning" on page 55 could form part of children's study programme. This will build their confidence for school work.

- ★ "The Magic Cave of Friends" on page 49 can be used if you sense any disharmony between friends in the classroom.

- ★ "Woodlands Healing" on page 45 is excellent for disruptive children or children who are feeling aggressive or out of control.

- ★ "The Beach and the Healing White Light" on page 52 works wonders with children who are sick or out of sorts.

- ★ "Flying in the Clouds" on page 59 is best used to ignite the imagination of your class. This helps them to access their creative minds and sets the scene for you to take them on to, perhaps, a creative writing task or a task that needs lots of ideas.

- ★ "The Pink Bubble" on page 64 is a very calming visualisation. It makes children feel safe and confident. This technique of creating a safe aura around oneself can be used effectively in the classroom on a day-to-day basis as well.

These visualisation exercises are an effective learning tool for teachers to use. You will find that children react very positively to these sessions and will look forward to their "quiet time" as much as you. Many children have used visualisation as a positive learning tool.

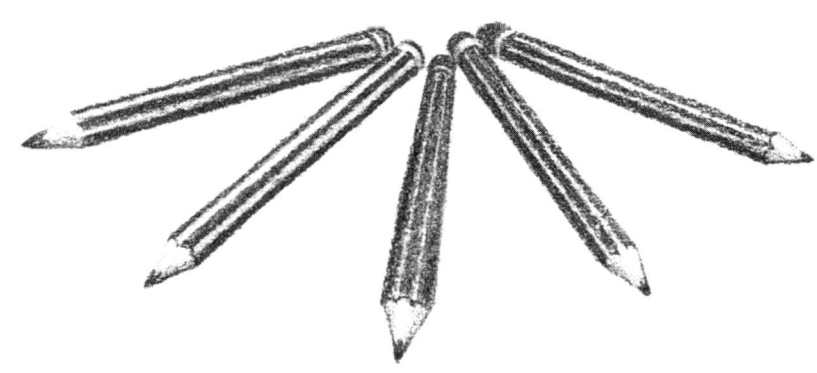

All Together Now

*Come into my dream garden,
Across the bridge of sleep ...*

Denise Linn

Success Stories

I have taught hundreds of children goalsetting and visualisation, and remember one group of seven-year-olds in particular. When they invited me into their classroom I sat on one of their small, elegant chairs and asked them to visualise a beautiful garden, to see the colours of the sky and the trees, and to walk over to a large inviting swing. This swing was covered in intertwining white flowers and when they sat down and held the ropes, the sweet, clear fragrance of the flowers hit their little noses like a thunderbolt of marvellous smell.

I asked the children to swing as high or as slowly as they wished. I explained that the swing understood what they wanted and magically gave it to them.

Every time they swung up they left any troubles they had behind and they felt better and better as they swung back and forth. They had no limits with their swinging, they could do whatever they wished.

I noticed that one of the girls, Primrose, was laughing with joy while she was doing the exercise and after the session I asked her what was so funny. Primrose said she could make her swing go so high that it circled over the top in a loop and was so much fun it made her squeal with laughter. So, visualisation is not limited in any way. You can create any bold or exciting thing you can think of in your imagination. Here are some stories of achievements children created by using visualisation and goalsetting.

Tammie

My daughter Tammie, who was six at the time, was having a lot of trouble riding the bike she received for Christmas. I would take her to the park and teach her to ride. Tammie was a little scared and it was not easy for me to help her because she wanted to ride all by herself. We would leave the park, both frustrated and unhappy, as Tammie was not able to ride her bike. One night, I said to Tammie that we would try something different for a week. Instead of practising at the park we would make a garden in our own imagination and practise there. So we did.

Instead of practising in the park Tammie used visualisation. She wrote down her goal, riding her bike, then drew a picture of herself riding her bike, then practised this in her imagination every night at bedtime. This visualisation became her special place for all her goals, her imaginary garden.

Every night at bedtime I asked Tammie to close her eyes and vividly imagine a beautiful garden, and in her imagination to paint pictures of how that garden looked. Once she could see the garden clearly, I asked Tammie to pretend her bicycle was there and to go over to it, pick it up and ride it easily and slowly. She did this for one week. The next Sunday

Tammie felt she could ride her bike in her imagination so well, she decided to go to the park and try again. I held the back of her bicycle seat while she got on and as her feet left the ground and reached the pedals, I knew that she had reached her goal.

She rode and rode and rode, without once falling off. Her dream came true.

She understood how easy it could be to learn new things in her imaginary garden and she still loves to go there every night.

Tammie is grown up now but when she goes to bed at night, she is very happy to go to her garden or special place to think about all her goals because she knows goalsetting and visualisation really works.

Name: Tammie		
Goal and drawing of goal	What I am prepared to give to get it	When I would like it by
To ride my bike by myself.	Practise riding my bike and feeling brave in my imagination every night.	Next week.

Cassie

Cassie had been using visualisation to go to sleep since she was a little girl. She had achieved so many things with it; making friends, losing her puppy fat, improving her schoolwork, becoming a strong swimmer.

Cassie was 15 years old when she decided she wanted to row in her school's first eight rowing crew. She had never even been in a boat. She desired it so strongly, it was all she could think about. She wrote her goal down in her dream book, she worked out how to increase her fitness level.

Every night as she went to sleep she imagined herself on the river in the boat with her crew rowing strongly and speedily down the river. She saw the wood of the boat, the depth of the river, the strong backs of the other rowers in front of and behind her.

She felt the pull of the oars in her hands, the strength of her body pulling the oars through the water. She, the other rowers, and the river were one.

Cassie created this dream every night for months, she trained to build her fitness level up, she tried out for the rowing crew.

She rowed in the first eight rowing crew for her school that year. Her dream came true.

Name: Cassie		
Goal and drawing of goal	What I am prepared to give to get it	When I would like it by
To row in the "first eight" rowing team at school.	To exercise to get fit. To practise being part of a team. Carry out my own training. Carry out my visualisation every night.	By the tryouts in June.

Ben

Ben was only five years old but a real worrier; he fretted about everything. So much so that every morning he would wake up with a wet bed.

This only made him feel worse as he was a big boy and wetting his bed was, to him, very babyish. His mother decided to use visualisation at bedtime with Ben. So Ben imagined himself strong and happy, playing happily with his friends, making decisions about what to do easily, and clearly. She also asked Ben to imagine waking up in the morning with a dry bed, bouncing out of bed happily and rushing to tell her about his dry bed and how very pleased he was about that.

It took five days to change the cycle. After five days Ben had stopped wetting his bed and was much more confident and happy. Ben uses his secret place to do all sorts of things now and believes that he has a safe place where he can go to achieve his dreams.

Name: Ben		
Goal and drawing of goal	What I am prepared to give to get it	When I would like it by
To wake up with a dry bed.	Practise making my own decisions.	By my birthday.
	See myself as strong and happy.	
	Every night, imagine waking up dry in the morning and running to tell Mum.	

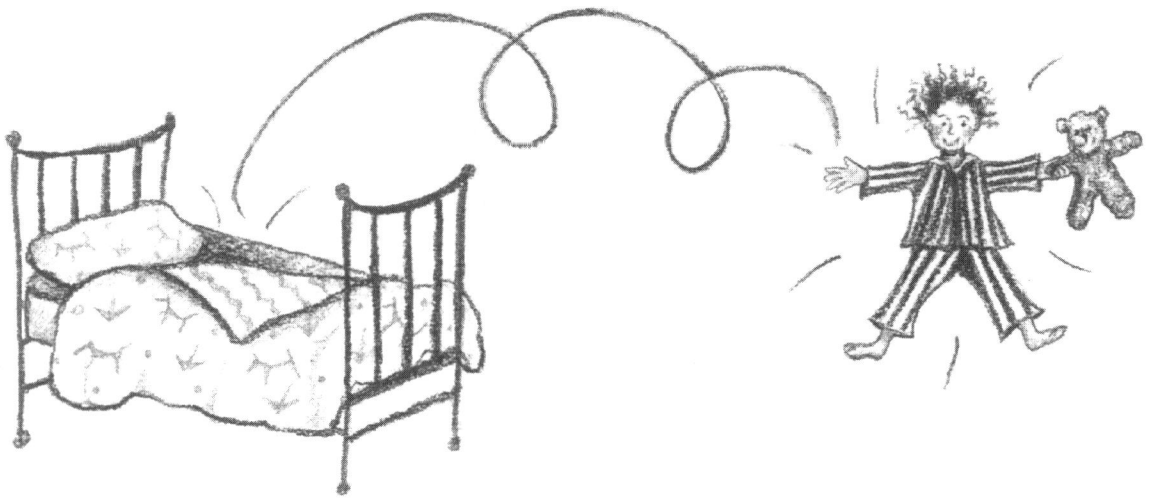

Sally

Catherine was immediately disliked when she swept into the classroom from a far-off country. Through her fear of a strange place, being the odd one out and her abrasive manner, she turned everyone in her class against her.

Sally was assigned to show her the ropes of the school. Sally is a kind-hearted child, always defending the underdog. However, everything she did for Catherine was refused, every kind gesture. But Sally didn't give up. Every night for a week she used visualisation to get to know Catherine better. She visualised them playing happily together, helping each other with their schoolwork and becoming firm friends.

Everyone in the classroom thought it was a miracle when Catherine began to be pleasant to Sally and then in turn to the other students, but Sally knew what had happened. She had believed in Catherine's friendship beforehand and through her visualisation had created the environment in her dreams for it to come true.

Name: Sally		
Goal and drawing of goal	What I am prepared to give to get it	When I would like it by
To be Catherine's friend.	Be nice to Catherine, even if she is unfriendly.	Next week.
To help Catherine make friends with the other children.	Imagine playing with Catherine in my secret garden every night.	Next week.

Now It's Your Turn

*Hold fast to dreams
For if dreams die
Life is a broken-winged bird
That cannot fly.*

LANGSTON HUGHES

How Visualisation Works

Everybody has an imagination. We use it to make things up and play games. We also use it to build things in the real world. All the things we achieve start as pictures in our imaginations, and so do our ideas about ourselves and other people and about things that haven't happened yet. How we imagine things helps to make them good or bad.

If someone imagines they will be car-sick on a long car trip or do badly in a test, what starts as an imaginary idea may end up with them really being car-sick or really doing badly in the test. Some grown-up people feel sick during difficult situations because when they were little they used to pretend they were sick when they wanted to get out of doing something. That's how powerful the imagination is.

So you see, you can use your imagination to make yourself a comfortable and a happy car traveller or to do really well at school, or find the courage to face things that you don't like.

People and visualisation

There are lots of people who use their imagination to fight disease or illness and lots of sporting people who use their imagination to become better runners or footballers or netball players. Lots of children use it for improving their school work, getting along better with their friends and parents, and improving their attitude to life.

They sit or lie down, relax, close their eyes and picture themselves just getting better and better at their sport, and their bodies and minds understand the pictures and become stronger and more successful.

There are many visualisation exercises you can share with children to open their creative minds.

Secret Garden

I'm going to take you to your own secret garden, where you can use your imagination in the best possible way. Start by making yourself comfortable, where you won't be disturbed, and then relax yourself. Let your arms and shoulders go wobbly and slowly close your eyes.

Feel yourself becoming more and more relaxed and comfortable. Now just imagine yourself standing in front of a beautiful garden door... it's your favourite colour and as you walk towards it, it opens slowly.

Behind the door is a beautiful garden, your own secret garden, and you can make this garden however you want it. You see your favourite flowers and trees, the sky is a beautiful clear blue. You can see your favourite animals, maybe your dog or your cat or your pony, and over in the corner is a beautiful, big swing.

This swing is covered with lovely white flowers. You sit on the swing and you swing easily and as high as you like. You don't need anyone to push you because in your imaginary garden everything is easy, so the swing pushes itself and stops itself also when you want it to.

Now I want you to stop your swing and move around the garden and look at the flowers and smell the different kinds of flowers and look at the different colours of the flowers and the different shapes.

Look, over there. There's a silky stream with clear cool water running over the soft sparkling pebbles. Put your feet in the running water, feel the softness of the water and the coolness on your skin. Now look around the garden and put anything else you like in that garden.

Now remember the times when you felt very good in your life, because that's what it's like here. Notice how good your body feels. When you think happy thoughts, your body feels so good. The funny thing is, when you think good things inside, things outside somehow go better for you. The world looks happier.

If you are happier inside, people seem to be nicer to you. Lessons seem easier, and more pleasant things seem to happen to you. So it's very important to learn how to use your imagination to change any bad feelings you have to good ones and to feel better about yourself and other people.

When you get these bad feelings (and everybody does, from time to time), there's a way you can get rid of these feelings in your imaginary garden. Go over to the stream and put your feet in the water. Now collect all these bad feelings in your middle, in your tummy, by tightening your body in a pretend ball and holding your breath for a count of one... two... three.

Now let your breath go and feel all those bad feelings leave your middle, go through your feet and flow away down the stream. The water carries your bad feelings down the stream... far away from you.

Imagine now that there is a beautiful grassy shady spot near that stream and you go over and lie down. While you are lying there, imagine anything you would like to change in the real world to make it better or happier.

If you are having trouble reading, you read perfectly in your garden. If you are having trouble with your homework, go over to your homework desk in your garden and see yourself doing your homework perfectly and easily and see your teacher smiling at you because she's so happy with your work. Everything is neat and correct in your homework book. Your handwriting is perfect in your garden.

Now think of other things that you wish to improve or change in your life. You may want to improve a sport, swimming or running, or you may want a new friend, or just a better friendship with someone special. If you do, I want you now to think about what you want, as if you've already received it, or are doing it really well.

The sun is shining in your garden and you feel warm and glowing with happiness. You feel lighter and freer. Now get up and skip and run happily around your garden.

When you use your imagination like this to talk to your body and feelings, it really works.

It is time to leave now and I want you to start walking towards the gate. As you leave, you know that you can come back whenever you like. And you can come here every night as you go to sleep. Now walk over and close the garden door behind you. You feel relaxed and happy and go to sleep (or gently open your eyes).

Woodlands Healing

There are many magical gardens. These places live in your head and your heart, and can be visited whenever you wish. One of my favourites is in the woodland.

You have to walk there by foot. It is not possible to drive there, so by the time you arrive you are a little short of breath, but full with the excitement of the beautiful walk to come. It is a warm and sunny day.

You can hear the sparrows singing their clear, pure music, you can smell the pine trees as you walk along the track. You can smell the sweet-smelling pink blossoms of the crab apple trees and see and feel the strength of a big English oak tree as you walk around and around it, just for fun.

There is an opening in the track and you look out of the clearing; and by surprise, you can see an ocean of yellow daffodils in the field below. The colour of the yellow is so creamy and rich that you want to run and jump in its beauty. You look up and today you see a clear electric blue sky that makes the yellow of the daffodils a very bright, bright yellow.

You leave the yellow daffodils and enthusiastically you stride down the track towards the tinkling sound of a babbling brook in the distance. As you are walking down the track, you notice the deep brown floor of the earth you walk on and feel the strength of the earth supporting you as you stride forward.

You notice the smells, the rich clean smells of the woods, the freshness climbs up your nostrils and you feel invigorated by the breath going in and out through your nose. Your eyes get accustomed to the greens of the trees around you and you notice how many shades of green there are. Some of the green leaves on the trees are almost green, some are deep blue-green, some are bottle-green like the green of the sea, some are gold and some are almost purple.

You need to go slower to take in all the beauty, you don't want to miss anything because it is a special place and you feel its specialness. You soak up the feeling of nature at work, you feel all the seasons at once and you feel mother earth and her very strong and powerful essence.

As you stride forwards, the sound of the water gets closer and you can almost smell the cleanness of the cascading water as it rushes to meet the river downstream. You feel excited because there is nothing quite as exciting as the taste and touch of the clear, clean, luxurious water to clean your throat, your heart and your soul. When you reach the brook you sit on a large white rock and you notice the velvety moss on the side of the rock, the side that does not see the sun, and you notice its vivid greenness.

As you cup your hands to collect the water, you feel how beautiful and clear the water is, and as it slides down your throat you feel it cleansing your body, your mind and your heart. It is taking all the fear away that you feel, of anything in your life that is making you sad and it is cleansing it and making it disappear. Like magic.

As you sit on the rock you let go of all the fear, the hate, and all the bad feelings you feel at the moment. You just let all your bad feelings tumble out, and down into the rush of the running water as you watch any sadness leave you. It is important to see the bad, negative feelings rushing away from you in the water, leaving you feeling clear and happy again.

Your eyes are still closed, and you feel light and free again. You feel the beauty of the babbling brook, still in your heart as you gently open your eyes and smile. You take the image of the luxurious woodlands with you back into your everyday life. You know that whenever you want to cleanse your fears, there is always the water from the brook in the woods you can visit to do this.

The Magic Cave of Friends

This is a very special night, as you are going to visit a mystical cave. Caves are very exciting because they hold such magic and intrigue. You are drawn to explore, you are inquisitive about what is in the cave, so you are excited about this journey.

You are closing your eyes now, and you are relaxing your body. You start at your feet. You wiggle your toes and relax your body, your legs feel light and free, your body slips into relaxation. Your head is free and ever so light, your eyes are peaceful and calm.

You are standing beside a boulder which hides the entrance to a white cave. The entrance is about as big as the front door to your house. You walk through the entrance and feel the darkness inside. Immediately your eyes grow accustomed to the cave and you see chandelier-like crystals hanging from the ceiling. They are blue and white stalactites, they are sparkling like Christmas fairy lights from the ceiling.

There is a large trunk in the corner of the cave with big hinges and you walk over to that trunk and with all your might you push open the lid. Inside this trunk are beautiful jewels and stones, wonderful old gold coins. Pretty and sparkling.

You feel the feeling of abundance, of having plenty, and it is a lovely feeling. You walk over to a bright, happy fire and sit down beside the fire and there is a wonderful story-teller there telling funny stories. Imagine all your friends are there with you, one by one around the campfire listening to the story-teller, all happy and pleased to be together. Everyone is laughing. You feel the closeness of your friends and the happiness in all laughing together. Look around your circle of friends and think of each of your friends' faces, their smiles, their eyes, their mouths. Think of each one individually.

As you sit around the fire I want you to feel your heart fill with love for all your friends. Imagine the place on the left side of your chest filled with the love you feel for your friends.

If you are having any trouble or problems with any of your friends, use this place around the fire to laugh and make peace with them again. Imagine you are sitting together and feeling safe and happy again.

Imagine the safeness of the cave, the warmth of the fire, the warmth of your friends, the warmth of your heart, and remember that whenever you are feeling unhappy with your friends there is a safe place where you can go to repair all the hurt you feel.

The Beach and the Healing White Light

The sky is clear and azure blue, as you sit on the beach. It is a wonderful summer day, the weather is warm but not hot; there is a faint, soft, cool breeze rustling your hair gently as you sit on the beach.

You have come here to be alone. Your family is relaxing and playing in the distance. They are near, but far away enough for you to be alone. You feel safe and warm.

You watch the waves roll onto the beach, you watch the fluffy surf spread its foamy layer of water across the sand. It has a rhythm, it makes you feel warm and safe to watch that rhythm repeat itself and the waves come in and go out, again and again.

The water is so clear. The blue of the water is crystal clean and clear with lighter blue closer to the shore, then gradually getting darker blue further out to sea.

You feel at peace with yourself, you close your eyes, you wiggle your toes in the sand and lie back into the envelope of warmth, into a soft bed of white clean sand.

MAKING DREAMS COME TRUE

As you lie there taking in the warmth of the beach, you imagine a clear white light coming through your body, through the top of your head. This white light fills your body, starting at your head and slowly going down your body, filling your face, your chest, your arms, your tummy, your legs, right down to your toes. You feel relaxed and cleansed.

Whenever you feel sick or in pain, you will always be able to heal yourself by remembering to bring this clean, clear, white light into your body. It makes you feel light and at peace with yourself.

Let the light float around your body, let it drift up and down your body warming every part of you inside. You can feel the white light inside you, you can feel the white light outside you as the sun warms you, lying on the beautiful white beach.

You are ready to leave the beach now, so you let the white light stay with you as you walk back to meet your family.

The Library of Learning

As you close your eyes you feel relaxed and very strong. You also feel very knowledgeable today, you feel as if you have the knowledge of many lifetimes within your brain. You are pleased that you feel this way because you are going to visit the library. It is a very special library, as it has everything you need to know in it and knowledge is easy to find, understand and use.

Before you open the door, notice your breathing, notice how rhythmic it is. Now take deep breaths, fill up your lungs with air, taking long, deep breaths, first your diaphragm and then all of your chest. Now release the air naturally and gently. Take three more of these long breaths, inhaling and exhaling with ease.

Now open the door to the library. You immediately notice that you are alone and the library is a small, intimate place, which you have totally to yourself. There is a very large table in the centre of the room, it is made out of very old dark timber.

It is a warm, welcoming table and you go over to it and sit down in a comfortable chair.

You look around and see all the shelves around you. They are stacked from floor to ceiling with books of all sizes and shapes and colours. There is even a high step-ladder so that you can easily reach the high shelves, which seem out of reach.

As you sit there at the library table you see all the wisdom of these books being absorbed by your wondrous brain. You can see all the ideas and words flying out of the books and being magnetised into your absorbent brain. Accept this wisdom, this knowledge, easily and readily.

Imagine now that you are sitting for an exam in this library. You are prepared for the exam and you are relaxed and calm. A teacher comes into the room and gently hands you the paper, she gives you a reassuring smile as she leaves. You are feeling very confident as you know that you have all the knowledge and understanding that you need to successfully complete this paper and to do extremely well in this exam.

You now close your eyes in the library and you see yourself receiving the best mark for this paper, and you see your teacher praising you for a job very well done. Now open your eyes in the library and begin the exam. Everything is flowing well, you understand all the questions and all the answers flow to you easily and freely.

You complete the paper and are very happy to see the teacher when she comes back because you are so pleased with your work.

Look around the library. You notice in one corner there is a music corner. All the musical instruments are there: a baby grand piano, a flute, a guitar, a cello, a saxophone, a violin, and your favourite instruments as well, all sparkling new and waiting to be played.

If you play or wish to play a musical instrument, go over to that corner and play the one of your choice with pleasure and ease. Enjoy the sound of the notes as you play every note perfectly, with understanding and sensitivity. Stay in the music corner and play perfectly, as long as you wish. (Be silent here if this child is enjoying playing and let them continue for one or two minutes, or until they become restless.)

You are now ready to leave the library, but you know that when you leave you will take all the wisdom and knowledge from the books, your success in your exams, and your musical genius with you. Take three long breaths, deeply filling your lungs, one... two... three. You feel confident, well and happy.

Flying in the Clouds

Gently close your eyes. You are lying in your garden, on a soft green bed of new grass. The smell is sweet and clean as you imagine that it has rained in your garden and the rain has left a superb, complete rainbow. It curves into your garden and looks as if it finishes right there, in your back garden. The colours of the rainbow are clear and bright.

Look at the brightness of the red. It is a fire engine red, so strong in colour. Orange is next, and you see that it is the orange like a tangerine, such a bright and happy colour.

Put your attention onto the yellow. See how the colour reminds you of the daffodils of spring. Around the daffodils is the strong support of the green leaves that protect them from the winds. That green is like the green of new leaves on the trees.

Now see and feel the healing colour of blue. It is like a clear summer day, sky-blue, and it fills your heart with love and kindness. Beside the blue is another type of blue, a deeper, stronger colour: indigo. It is a fascinating colour because you don't see it very much - it is like a deep purple but not as strong. Then imagine a little bunch of violets. This is the last but the most beautiful of the colours in your rainbow.

Now that you have taken the colours into your mind and heart, visualise lifting yourself off the ground and floating in mid air. You are rising higher into the sky, and as you do this you gently roll over and notice that you are about 50 metres above the ground and you are gently moving. Yes, you are flying. Like a very graceful bird. It is effortless. All you need to do is move your arms slightly from side to side and you can change direction.

You glide easily over your garden. You notice just how wonderful your garden is from the air, how everything looks so neat and full of life.

You decide to venture further afield, you decide to visit Africa. As you glide over the grassy terrain you see all the animals you have read about in books: elephants standing in groups near their watering hole, leopards running swiftly through the jungle, monkeys high up in their trees scratching their backs and twirling their tails. You see the giraffe, tall and sleek. You circle the giraffe and notice its orange/ochre coloured fur with the black spots in no particular order, covering its body. It is a wonderful feeling being able to see the giraffe in your imagination. You feel strong and free, you feel that you can do anything, go anywhere.

You leave Africa and decide to fly to the Grand Canyon in North America. Its beauty is breathtaking. The best way to see the Grand Canyon is by air and you take advantage of being able to fly by sweeping up and down the mountains, looking into all the caves hidden to the naked eye from the ground, but you can see them all very, very clearly.

You watch with wonderment at the endless size of the Grand Canyon. The valleys are breathtakingly beautiful, and the mountains so huge and imposing by comparison. It takes your breath away.

You decide to leave the sweeping beauty of the canyon and, because you can fly you decide to visit a place that you have always wanted to visit. This may be a far-off land, it may be in Europe, it may be in the next town.

You want to go there to explore, so you gently fly to this special place and you do and see whatever you have desired to do and see. I will stop talking now so that you can visit this very special place all by yourself.

(After about two to three minutes, or when the child becomes restless, continue reading.)

Now that you have visited all of these exciting places, come back to your garden, notice how everything is in order, just how you left it, and slowly and softly land. Nestle back onto the soft grass and now that you have finished your daring adventure, relax and let go, knowing that you can visit anywhere in the universe by flying there yourself.

The Pink Bubble

Imagine that you are walking in your favourite garden. Everything around you is colourful and abundant, all the trees are straight and tall, the grass has just been freshly mown and smells fresh and green. As you walk, you notice that everything has a vibrating band of light around it. This is an aura. The trees have a very strong white light surrounding them, protecting them. You notice that the birds have a blue light, about the length of your finger, surrounding each one. You can only see the blue light when you are feeling calm and confident. You feel calm and confident today.

Stroll around your garden and notice that all the living, growing things in your garden have an aura of some sort around them. Some have a strong clear colour, some a vibrating white light, some just a hint of shadow, but everything has an aura. Everything.

Now lie down under a shady tree. Look up at the bright sky. It is azure blue and fills your heart. The sun is shining brightly and you feel full of warmth and happiness.

Imagine as you are lying there that you surround yourself with a pink bubble. It covers all of your body, front and back. It is about your hand's width all around you, enveloping you in a warm glow. This is the pink bubble of love and you can surround yourself with it whenever you wish.

If you are going on a long trip and wish to be safe, surround yourself and the car with the bubble and you will feel protected for your journey.

When you leave your house for your trip, surround your room, your things and the complete house with a pink bubble of love, protecting it while you are away.

When you finish your exam and pass in the paper to your teacher, surround this with your bubble. When posting a letter to a friend or relative, post it with a big pink bubble of love.

Surrounding the things you love with this bubble helps you to overcome any fear or anxiety you may have about what you are doing and it really works.

Now visualise your family one by one and put a pink bubble around each one. (Allow a minute for this to be done.) Then visualise your friends with this bubble around them. (Another minute here.) Now a large bubble around your house so all is safe and happy within your home.

As you open your eyes you know that whenever you feel fear or hurt, or just when you want to feel safe, you can put a pink bubble of love around whatever you need to and it will make you feel loved and protected.

Achieving Your Dreams

*Do not be too timid and squeamish about your actions.
All life is an experiment.*

RALPH WALDO EMERSON

Goalsetting

When you daydream or think about things that you would like to happen, you may be surprised to find the things you think about very often come true. You can help this daydream process by setting goals.

Goalsetting is used with visualisation to direct your dreams into action, and action is about how and what you are prepared to do to achieve that dream. When you write a goal down you activate a part of your brain that says "thank you for the written instruction" and arranges your behaviour to achieve this instruction.

When you go to do the shopping you take a list with you of all the things you need. A special part of your brain methodically organises your activities to get everything on that list. So it's very important to activate all of your brain by writing your goals down on a piece of paper and working out what you are prepared to do to get the goal. For instance, if you want to improve a relationship with someone you will need to speak to them nicely so that your behaviour matches your goal.

If you want to improve your time for running a 50 metre sprint you will have to be prepared to go to training every day. If you would like to learn to play the cello you will need to remember to bring the cello home from school three times a week to practise for an hour after dinner.

It is also important to activate the brain with a timeframe. By setting a time when you would like to achieve the goal you will activate the part of the brain that loves a deadline. When did you get your assignment in? When did you let your friend know if you were coming over? Usually you or your teacher set a deadline to do the assignment and usually you end up doing it by that time. So by setting a timeframe you are giving yourself your best chance of achieving that goal.

It is sometimes hard to imagine how long something will take, so it may help you to make your own calendar. Try making it like an advent calendar, which counts down to the special time you have chosen. Instead of counting down to Christmas, you will count from the beginning of your visualisation to when the timeframe you have set yourself ends.

In your special calendar make space for revising your goals regularly as well as the nightly visualisation exercises. Add some highlights and exciting things too. How will you celebrate when you are halfway there! Leave a blank or two because something might happen that you want to record. At the end, add another space for checking your progress because you might want to make a revision. This is your calendar, so make the most of it.

You will have lots of goals, lots of dreams that you would like to come true. Think for a moment. If you would like to have a friendship with someone, write down that person's name and how you would like your relationship with that person to be. Would you like to be better at your schoolwork, or swimming, or singing? Or you might like to be brave enough to go on the school bus by yourself. Anything that you have a strong feeling about, anything that you would like to achieve, can become a goal.

Kylie's goals

Kylie was a very shy, awkward girl who really just wanted one best friend, but it was hard for her to make friends. She started talking to Jodie while walking to school one day and they found out that they had a love for horses. It was this passion in common that directed Kylie to get out her goal book that night and dream in goal form.

Kylie wanted to be friends with Jodie so she wrote down Jodie's name. Then she wrote down what kind of friendship she would like to have and how she thought she could make her dream come true. She also wrote down how long she thought it might take.

It is very important to write down what you will do or what you are prepared to give to make this goal happen, because it doesn't work as well without doing this.

Kylie wrote down her goals, how she would make them happen and how long it might take. Then she drew a picture of them.

Name: Kylie		
Goal and drawing of goal	What I am prepared to give to get it	When I would like it by
I would like my friend Jodie to like me and for us to be friends.	I will always speak nicely to her. I will visualise happily playing with her in my cave every night.	Next week.

Kylie and Jodie became good friends.

How to Set Goals

To set your goals, think very clearly about how you would like your life to be, what you would like to happen in your life, then write these goals down on paper, in the order that you would like them to happen.

Writing down your goals is easy, but sometimes you may need some help. If you feel comfortable about it, talk with a friend or adult who understands goalsetting and ask them to help you. Here are some simple steps to help you to prepare your goalsetting chart and to use visualisation to make your dreams come true.

FIND a quiet place somewhere where you can think about all the wonderful things you would like to have happen to you.

THINK about how you would like each part of your life to be. What are the nice things you would like to happen? What are the things you would like to learn? These are your own personal dreams.

WRITE down your dreams on your goalsetting chart. These are your goals now.

DECIDE what you need to do to make each goal come true. What will you do to make it happen? Write these activities down on your goalsetting chart.

WRITE down when you would like each goal to be achieved. It could be tomorrow, next week, or next year. You might like to use other ways of counting time - try before your birthday, before Christmas or any other time that is meaningful to you.

DRAW a picture of your goal. Drawing pictures of your goals is important because you can see more clearly what you want. If, like Kylie, you wanted a special friend, you would draw a picture of yourself and your friend with your arms around each other smiling and being friends.

READ your goals out loud once a day. This will help them come true.

VISUALISE your goals. Close your eyes as you are going to sleep at night and go to your special place, your garden, your cave, your river bank or your beach and imagine as vividly as you can all the goals you have written down really happening.

CONGRATULATE yourself for gaining what you have achieved so far. Feel good about your achievements.

REVISE your goals every month.

Things to Remember When Making Goals

An important part of achieving your goals is being nice to others and nice to yourself. When you are nice to others, it makes the world such a beautiful place because it makes the people you are nice to happy and they in turn are nice to others. So you can see it is like a circle and eventually it comes back to you.

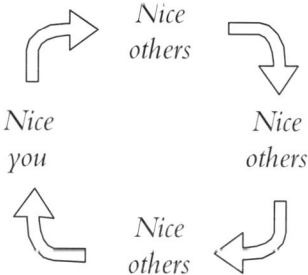

Of course, some things you can't change. If someone is dead or has gone away, it is not possible for them to come back.

Most things you can change, though. You can change the way you feel about yourself and others. You can change the results you get for your subjects at school or how you achieve in sport. You can change your relationship with your mother or father, stepmother or stepfather.

Sandy's story

Recently I helped a young girl called Sandy set her goals and action plan ("What I Am Prepared to Give to Get It" on the goalsetting chart). She was having a very hard time getting on with her stepfather. Her stepfather had come into her life not by her design but by her mother's. He believed he had the right to tell her what and when to do things, he took up all of her beautiful mother's time and left little time for her mother to spend with her. He was always grumpy, especially when he came home from work. He worked as an ambulance driver and when he came home at night he was always short with her, pushing her away, telling her to go to her room, needing to be alone, away from the kids for a while.

Whenever she did anything for him or her mother, he was always critical. He seemed always too hard to please. Sandy decided to set a goal about her stepfather and work out what she was prepared to give to get it. She knew in her heart of hearts that if she did not take action about the relationship, it would only get worse. Brave girl! This is what she did. What Sandy was prepared to give, she believed, would give her the behaviour that would help her to turn the tide with her stepfather.

Name: Sandy – First Goal		
Goal and drawing of goal	What I am prepared to give to get it	When I would like it by
I will get on well with my stepfather.	To stand back from the situation when I am being criticised and detach myself and not attack back.	By Christmas this year.
	To offer to help more around the house, to be the first to offer to help.	
	To stay out of the arguments that the other children have with him, let them sort it out with him directly.	
	To stop the hate I feel for him in my head, to visualise liking him and getting on well.	

Last time I spoke with her she looked like a new person. Her posture was more erect, her confidence had changed for the better, everything about her had matured. She was beaming. Yes, she had improved her relationship with her stepfather. He was still grumpy and irritable sometimes but, she said, he was treating her with much more respect, concern and interest.

She was most pleased about her improved relationship with her mother. Her mother had seen just how much she had changed her attitude and was enormously proud and grateful for her support. Somehow they had become allies and friends again and this made Sandy so very happy.

Sandy showed her mother her goal sheet and they decided to do this goalsetting together every four weeks, to review it and reset goals regularly. If it could work with Sandy's relationship with her stepfather they firmly believed that it could work with any goals.

Revising goals

You need to revise your goals every month, because you might need a little more time or to try a different approach.

When Sandy revised her list at Christmas she found she needed to change her action plan – 'What I Am Prepared to Give to Get It' – on the goalsetting chart. She was making progress with her stepfather but it was very hard to break her old relationship pattern with him and this is how she decided to do it:

Name: Sandy – Revised Goal		
Goal and drawing of goal	What I am prepared to give to get it	When I would like it by
I will have a positive relationship with my stepfather.	I will visualise every night my positive relationship with my stepfather. To support my stepfather in thought, in deed. To respect my mother's and his relationship. To let go of the past and look forward to a more positive future. To visualise our family happy and harmonious.	By my birthday in April.

You see, her goals were not unrealistic, they just had some unrealistic timeframes.

Bobby's goals

Bobby's goalsetting chart worked well. He was pleased with his goals and was beginning to feel more confident at school. When he looked back at his goalsetting chart, he found that he could make them clearer and easier to work out.

Name: Bobby		
Goal and drawing of goal	What I am prepared to give to get it	When I would like it by
I would like to be better.	I will try harder at school work.	By the end of first term.
	I will imagine doing well at school in my Library of Learning every night at bedtime.	

He changed his goals to make them more specific. He also thought about how long he would need to make his dreams come true. He then made the timeframe more realistic.

MAKING DREAMS COME TRUE

Name: Bobby		
Goal and drawing of goal	What I am prepared to give to get it	When I would like it by
I would like to understand the words I read in books.	Read one extra book with my father every night. Visualise myself looking up new words in the dictionary.	Before the beginning of second term.
To improve my maths so I can do all my homework.	Ask more questions of Mrs Marsh.	By the end of first term.
To gain an A+ in my exams.	Visualise doing well in my exams in my Library of Learning every night at bedtime.	For my third term report card.

Your Turn

Now it is your turn to write down all the things you would like to happen in your life. If you would like to be better at your school work, write down exactly how you would like to improve and what you are happy to do to make it happen. Here are some examples of goals:

Name: Write your name here		
Goal and drawing of goal	What I am prepared to give to get it	When I would like it by
Swim in the school swimming team.	Go to training every morning. Go to my garden swimming pool and visualise winning my race at inter-house swimming.	By mid term.
To ride my bike.	Practise every day. Visualise every night in my garden.	Next week.

I will play the cello.	Borrow the cello from the music room and practise my pieces.	By the end of year concert.
	Visit my Library of Learning in my imagination and play the cello every night.	
To play a part in the school play, and play it well.	Try out for all parts and practise every day.	By the end of the term.
	Visualise the play every night with me in the lead role.	
To be able to speak clearly and fluently.	Do my speaking exercises in the morning.	After Christmas.
	See myself in my garden speaking in the classroom.	

Your goals

Write your own goals on this special page.
Remember:

- ★ Your name
- ★ Goal and drawing of goal
- ★ What you are prepared to give to get it
- ★ When you would like it by.

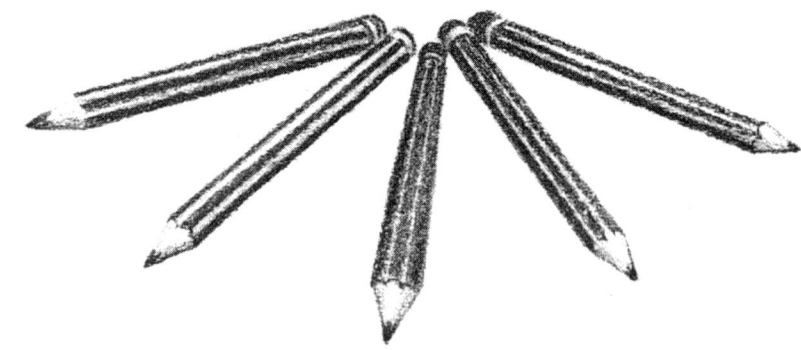

Now you are ready to make your dreams come true.

MAKING DREAMS COME TRUE

Name:		
Goal and drawing of goal	What I am prepared to give to get it	When I would like it by

The author and publishers grant permission for multiple copies of this page for non-commercial classroom use.

Name:		
Goal	What I am prepared to give to get it	When I would like it by

The author and publishers grant permission for multiple copies of this page for non-commercial classroom use.

Making Dreams Come True

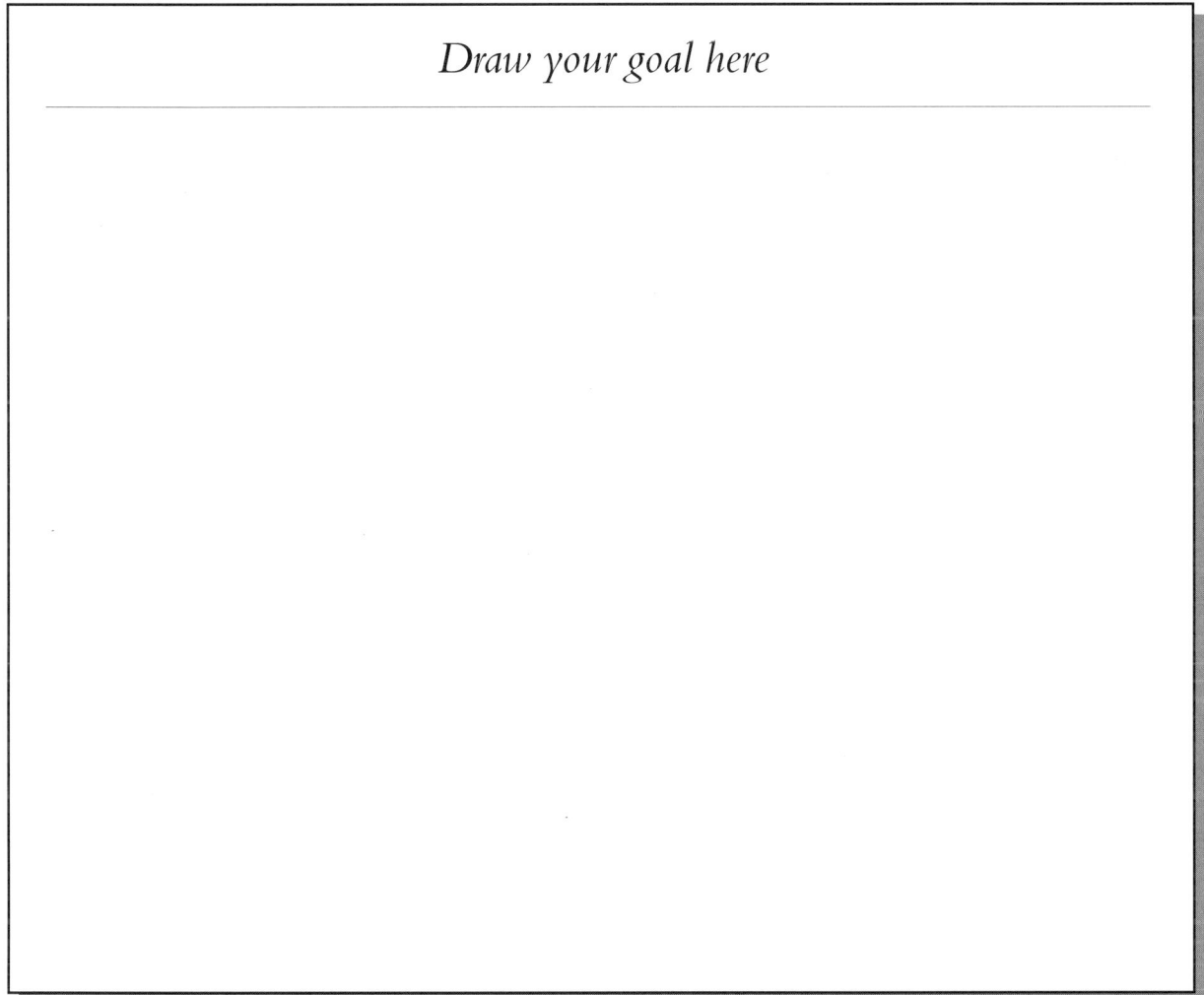

Draw your goal here

The author and publishers grant permission for multiple copies of this page for non-commercial classroom use.

Your Own Special Place for Dreams

*As I travel through this lifetime,
swimming down the stream
I pick up many baubles, people, places, things.
The one thing I'll take with me
when I leave the stream isn't any bauble,
It's a pocketful of dreams.*

KARL BETTINGER

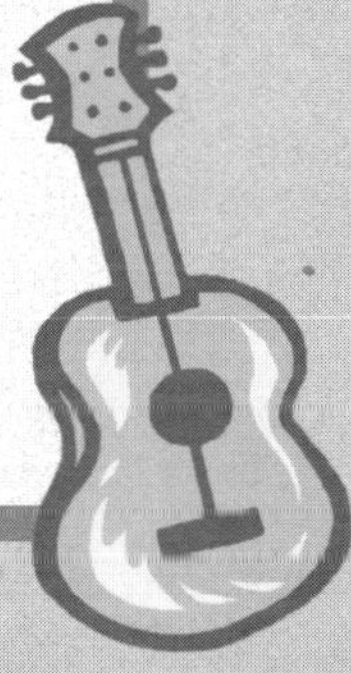

Keep on Dreaming

Just before you go to sleep at night and again as soon as you wake up, think about your goals. The more you think about them, the more they will come true. So see yourself with your friend, see yourself winning the prize for swimming or reading. See who is with you, imagine the whole picture. Imagine it as you would like it to happen and make it as colourful and exciting as you can.

Visualisation is a very important part of goalsetting. Use the exercises in the front of the book, make them more personal by adding your own ideas and goals. Or you may create your own special place for your goals.

If you have a garden (or any special place) where you like to go in your imagination to think about your goals, make a drawing of it.

Remember always to have nice happy goals and a beautiful happy place where you can learn wonderful things, so you will always have a beautiful place to go at night just before going to sleep.

Row, row, row your boat,
Gently down the stream,
Merrily, merrily, merrily, merrily,
Life is but a dream.

MAKING DREAMS COME TRUE

www.dreamlife.co.uk

Praise for Making Dreams Come True

When I go to my magic garden and dream my goals, I know I will be safe.
        LAUREN, AGED 6

This is a very soothing book. It helps you to relax and to focus on what you really want to do. It has helped me to believe that I can achieve my goals if I try.
        JAMES WILLIAM DONNELLY, AGED 9

Goal setting and motivation are extremely important aspects of education. The visualisation techniques described in this book could help teachers and parents tap into children's imaginative resources and help develop their self esteem, confidence and positive outlook on life.
        ANNETTE ENGLISH, SENIOR EDUCATIONAL PSYCHOLOGIST

Good mental preparation goes hand-in-hand with good physical preparation. Developing your ability to control what you think, and how you see yourself, rehearsing, focusing, refocusing away from distractions, is part of preparing for competition. "Making Dreams Come True" is a book that will help you to perform to your best and achieve your goals.
        BARRIE BURKE, CHIEF ROWING COACH

We can set ourselves goals and through a planned approach we might achieve our targets, but with visualisation we can turn "might" into "will".
        SALLY COLE, HEADTEACHER, MICKLETON COUNTY PRIMARY SCHOOL

Believe you can't do something - immediately you create a barrier between you and your goal. Believe you can - immediately the barrier disappears, leaving you closer to your goal and open to achieving it. Add appliance and determination and enjoy the journey of achieving.
        JAYNE ASHBOURNE, ACTRESS, ROYAL SHAKESPEARE COMPANY

Before a race I visualise the challenge. I see myself getting my best start, then my best technique, and my best power finish to win. If you can see yourself doing what you want to do you can achieve anything.
        ALICE SALT, JUNIOR SCULLER, STRATFORD-UPON-AVON BOAT CLUB